Montreal & Quebec Travel Guide

The Most Up-to-Date Pocket Guide to Discover Montreal & Quebec's Hidden Gems and Plan an Unforgettable Journey in Canada's Francophone Heartland

David Smith

© Copyright 2023 - All rights reserved.

The contents of this book may not be reproduced, duplicated, or transmitted without the direct written permission of the author or publisher.

Under no circumstances will the publisher or author be held liable for any damages, recovery, or financial loss due to the information contained in this book. Neither directly nor indirectly.

Legal Notice:

This book is protected by copyright. This book is for personal use only. You may not modify, distribute, sell, use, quote, or paraphrase any part or content of this book without the permission of the author or publisher.

Disclaimer Notice:

Please note that the information contained in this document is for educational and entertainment purposes only. Every effort has been made to present accurate, current, reliable, and complete information. No warranties of any kind are stated or implied. The reader acknowledges that the author is not offering legal, financial, medical, or professional advice. The contents of this book have been taken from various sources. Please consult a licensed professional before attempting any of the techniques described in this book.

By reading this document, the reader agrees that under no circumstances will the author be liable for any direct or indirect loss arising from the use of the information contained in this document, including but not limited to - errors, omissions, or inaccuracies.

Table of Contents

Introduction..6

Chapter 1: Travel Essentials.......................9

Brief History about Montreal........................... 9

Why Choose Montreal 11

A Quick Snapshot of Montreal's Vibe............................. 13

Chapter 2: Must Visit Places in Montreal.................... 21

Chapter 3: Itineraries.................................32

The Five-Day Exploration Itinerary............................. 32

The One-Week Itinerary 34

The Weekend Getaway................................ 35

Chapter 4: Best Restaurants and Cuisine in Montreal
....36

Time Out Market Montreal 41

Chapter 5: Accommodations in Montreal 44

Chapter 6: Romantic Things to do in Montreal 50

Time to Get Romantic 51

Romantic Things to do in Quebec City........................... 54

Feel the Love 55

Interesting Getaways Based On Your Budget 57

Not-so-costly romance 58

Exceptionally big for a small pocket 59

Chapter 7: Cultural Activities in Montreal 60

Major Festivals in Greater Montréal 60

Cultural Venues in Greater Montréal 64

Museums and art galleries 65

Cultural Communities in Greater Montréal 66

Privileged Access Programs 66

Cultural Offerings in Suburban Areas 68

Chapter 8: Nightlife And Festivals In Montreal 71

Cultural Festivals 79

Chapter 9: Souvenirs And Shopping in Montreal 90

Artisan Jewelry 91

Other Interesting Souvenirs from Canada: 96

Chapter 10: Tips For Traveling in Montreal 98

Is Montréal worth visiting? 98

Tips for Your First Trip to Montreal 99

Introduction

Imagine the thrill of stepping onto the cobblestone streets of Old Montreal, a place where echoes of the 17th century blend seamlessly with the vibrant energy of a modern metropolis. Picture yourself immersing in the grandeur of Notre-Dame Basilica, a place where past and present coexist to offer an experience unlike any other in the world. This is Montreal, the second-largest French-speaking city in the world, and it is waiting to be discovered. But why stop there? Extend your journey to Quebec City, where timeless charm, captivating natural wonders, and exquisite culinary delights promise an adventure of a lifetime.

Sounds exciting, doesn't it? But we understand the daunting task of planning such a journey, the uncertainties, and the questions flooding your mind. What to see? Where to dine? How to navigate through these cities like a local, and how to make the most of your time in these cultural hubs? Whether you're a first-time visitor or a seasoned traveler, these are valid concerns that could turn a potential thrilling adventure into a stressful ordeal. But worry not, this is where this book, "Montreal and Quebec Travel Guide 2023," comes in.

This guide is your trusted companion, meticulously designed to help you conquer the anxieties that come with exploring new territories. It promises an insider's look into the heart of these cities, highlighting their captivating wonders, best dining experiences, and must-see attractions, ensuring your journey is memorable and seamless. We have devoted hours to mapping out easy navigation routes, pinpointing hidden gems, and selecting the best accommodations for every budget. This book is your comprehensive roadmap, walking you through your journey from start to finish.

The authors of this guide are seasoned travel experts who have traversed the length and breadth of Montreal and Quebec City, exploring their nooks and crannies, tasting their cuisines, and living their cultures. Their intimate knowledge of these cities is distilled in these pages, offering you a firsthand guide to experiencing these cities like a local. In their hands, you're guaranteed an authentic, enriching experience.

So, why this book? Well, we believe in the power of immersion, the magic that happens when you go beyond the beaten path, explore new territories, and connect with cultures. That is what

"Montreal and Quebec Travel Guide 2023" offers - an opportunity to immerse yourself in the beauty and diversity of Montreal and Quebec City, guided by people who know these cities inside out.

Therefore, if you seek an extraordinary journey, one where you explore not as a tourist but as a discerning traveler, this book is for you. Embark on this journey with us, as we unravel the vibrant mosaic of cultures, gastronomy, and history that makes Montreal and Quebec City truly enchanting destinations. Your adventure awaits, and this guide is your first step towards it.

Chapter 1:
Travel Essentials

Brief History about Montreal

The second-largest city in Canada, Montreal, is located in the province of Quebec and has a nearly 8,000-year-old history. The indigenous St. Lawrence Iroquoians who lived in the region before European settlers came set the stage for the present tale. Jacques Cartier, the first European explorer in the area, arrived in Montreal in 1535 while looking for a route to Asia during the Age of Exploration.

As a part of a plan to construct a French colonial empire, Ville Marie Fortress was built in 1642. This community swiftly developed into a hub for the fur trade and a base for French incursions into New France. However, Montreal didn't receive official city status until 1832. The completion of the Lachine Canal and the city's tenure as the United Province of Canada's capital from 1844 to 1849 both contributed to this period of tremendous growth. The largest city in British North America and the cultural and economic center of Canada by 1860 was Montreal.

Between 1883 and 1918, the absorption of nearby villages caused another change in the city's personality, turning Montreal once more into a city with a Francophone majority. Although the Great Depression caused great hardship and unemployment, it was also during this time that the city's first skyscrapers began to rise.

Montreal suffered greatly as a result of World War II, which resulted in conscription, protests, and the 1944 Conscription Crisis. Early in the 1950s after the war, the city's population had topped one million, and its infrastructure had grown to include a new metro system and a larger harbor.

Montreal is one of the North American epicenters of Francophone culture today and a significant industrial, commercial, and financial powerhouse. It is praised internationally and regarded as one of the world's best cities. The city's vibrant culture and rich history are intermingled and serve as a monument to the fortitude and diversity of its residents.

Why Choose Montreal

There are several strong reasons to pick Montreal as a travel destination in 2023. You should put Montreal on your travel itinerary this year for the following reasons:

1. **Cultural Blend**: The heart of Canadian culture, Montreal skillfully combines French and Canadian elements in its architecture, way of life, and food. With its cobblestone streets and old structures, the city can give you the impression that you are in Europe, but around every corner, you will see modern skyscrapers that reflect the city's metropolitan side.

2. **Diverse Attractions**: The city has a wide variety of attractions, something for every kind of traveler, from verdant green parks to ancient basilicas and inventive art galleries. For instance, Mont Royal, which was created by the same individual who created Central Park in New York City, provides breathtaking panoramic views of the city and mountains. The early 17th-century Old Montreal neighborhood is home to well-known structures including the Notre-Dame Basilica and Montreal Science Centre, as well as restaurants serving food with a taste of 1700s Quebec.

3. **Food Scene**: Montreal is renowned for having a vibrant and delectable cuisine scene. You'll discover a wide variety of alternatives to please your palate, whether you're

seeking for French-inspired cuisine or a more global menu.

4. **Historical Charm**: History aficionados may explore cobblestone lanes and antique greystone buildings that date back to the 1700s in the city's Old Town, which resembles something straight out of medieval France. It's fun to wander through Antique Montreal, where you can also see significant sites like the Place des Armes, which houses the city's first seminary and other old structures.

5. **Outdoor Activities**: In and around Montreal, there are numerous bike paths, hiking trails, and mountains for outdoor enthusiasts to explore.

6. **Budget-Friendly**: In addition, Montreal is regarded as being far less expensive than other significant Canadian cities, making it a desirable location for travelers on a tight budget.

7. **Environmentally Conscious Travel**: The city also promotes environmentally friendly travel, offering alternatives to calculate and offset your carbon footprint through funding research on carbon sequestration and tree planting. This makes it a fantastic option for tourists that care about the environment.

Montreal is a desirable travel destination for 2023 with its dynamic blend of culture, history, food, outdoor activities, and eco-friendly possibilities.

A Quick Snapshot of Montreal's Vibe

Montreal, the second most populous city in Canada, is a thriving metropolis that blends the best of North American culture with European charm. It's a city brimming with a lively energy, attractive to tourists for its diverse cuisine, rich history, verdant parks, and vibrant arts scene. Montreal has something for everyone and boasts a unique vibe that sets it apart from other cities.

This vibrant city is undoubtedly the cultural beating heart of Canada, teeming with lush green parks, historic basilicas, and innovative art galleries that are unique to North America. One of its key selling points is its food scene. Food is woven tightly into Montreal's culture, where traditional favorites meet modern culinary innovations. Whether you're a food enthusiast or a casual eater, Montreal's gastronomy scene will likely satiate your cravings.

Architecturally, Montreal presents an alluring fusion of the old and the new. Walk down the city's European-style cobblestone alleys, turn the corner, and you'll be greeted by towering skyscrapers and metropolitan high rises. Old Montreal (or Vieux-Montreal) is the heart of the city, featuring the spectacular Notre-Dame Basilica, one of North America's largest churches, and other attractions that offer a taste of Quebec from the 1700s.

Montrealers adore their festivals, hosting over 100 throughout the year, making the city a year-round destination filled with events that cater to various interests. Besides, it's called "The City of Festivals" for a reason, which makes it a hub of cultural diversity and lively entertainment.

Visitors can also expect plenty of outdoor experiences. For example, the city's massive park, Mount Royal, is loved by locals and tourists alike for its splendid views and recreational attractions. Despite its size, it never feels crowded, offering a serene respite amidst the bustling city.

Montreal's vibe is a delightful amalgamation of rich history, diverse food, lush green parks, fervor for festivals, and stunning architecture. Whether you're a history buff, a food lover, an art enthusiast, or a nature lover, Montreal's charm is sure to captivate you.

How To Get There And Moving Around

In addition to its diverse appeal, distinctive architecture, and vibrant food scene, Montreal is renowned for its effective and reasonably priced public transportation system. Getting around Montreal on a budget is fairly doable, whether you're a local or a visitor, and many would agree that using the metro is even more efficient and enjoyable than attempting to navigate the city's always shifting detours by automobile.

The STM subway system is your best option if you intend to stay in Old Montreal, Le Plateau, or the downtown area. The metro system is spotless, dependable, and extensive; it encircles the whole downtown area of Montreal and extends into parts of its suburbs, including Lasalle, Laval, and the South Shore. There are just four lines in the system, which links the downtown area to popular tourist destinations, bus terminals, and railway stations.

A single metro journey costs $3.50 CAD, or you can get two tickets for $6.50 CAD. Day passes can be purchased for $10. The nighttime pass, which is unrestricted until 5 a.m. and only costs $5.50, is an option if you want to commute primarily after 6 p.m. Children under the age of 11 ride free.

On weeknights, the Montreal Metro operates from 5:30 a.m. to 12:30 a.m., and on weekends, it operates until 1:30 a.m. The evening service is less frequent, with up to a 10-15 minute wait for a train starting at 9 p.m. During peak hour, you can anticipate catching a train every 3-5 minutes.

One bus transfer is included in a single fare, however re-entry into the metro is not. You won't have to pay another fare if you're changing metro lines unless you leave the station. Transfer stations are clearly identified and accessible without travelling above ground. Although many have small gaps between the platform and the train, making it easier for people to approach and disembark, not all metro stations are wheelchair accessible.

Every metro line offers wheelchair-accessible seating, and all stops have a combination of voice and visual announcements.

Montreal provides additional transportation options in addition to its public transportation system. You can utilize a BIXI public bike to travel around some of the city's 750 kilometers of bike trails or you can explore the neighborhoods of Montreal on foot. You could even take a boat out on the St. Lawrence and enjoy the beauty of the city. Last but not least, there are also automobile and taxi services if you want something more private.

Whatever your favorite method of transportation, Montreal has a range of options to make your stay as convenient and pleasurable as possible.

Best Seasons to Visit Montreal and Corresponding Activities

Every season in Montreal, a city renowned for its vibrant festivals and gorgeous architecture, is appealing and offers visitors a range of activities and a distinct flavor.

Winter Activities

There are lots of fun things to do if you decide to go throughout the winter (late November to early March). You can make your own snow using hair conditioner and baking soda, or you can participate in a DIY science project by making a snowstorm in a jar, both of which are inspired by the activities stated in the source. Additionally, Montreal is well-known for its winter celebrations, including Montreal en Lumière and the outdoor winter carnival Fête des Neiges, which both feature light shows, fine cuisine, and outdoor activities.

Spring Activities

You can visit the city's lovely parks in the spring, from mid-April to May, when they are in full bloom, such as Mount Royal Park and the Botanical Garden. Kids might take part in a rain cloud painting exercise as stated in the source, which would make it entertaining and informative. The Bal en Blanc, an electronic music festival that often occurs over the Easter weekend, is another event held in Montreal.

You can hike, establish a miniature garden, have a picnic in one of Montreal's many parks, or go to a farm to meet young animals, all of which can be done while drawing inspiration from the source.

Summer Activities

A great season to enjoy the city's outdoor pursuits is the summer, which lasts from June to August. During this period, Montreal's festival calendar is also in full flow. As stated in the source, you can engage in fond memories in one of Montreal's parks by playing tag, blowing bubbles, or having a water balloon war. For foodies, enjoying a BBQ or sampling various summer fruits at a nearby farmer's market might be fun. The Jazz Festival, Just For

Laughs Comedy Festival, and Les FrancoFolies de Montréal, the largest Francophone festival in the world, are all held in Montreal during the summer.

Whatever time of year you decide to come, Montreal gives visitors of all ages a plethora of adventures, a chance to immerse themselves in the local culture, and a lot of fun.

General Packing

Clothing, toiletries, medical supplies, electronic devices, and power adapters that fit Canadian outlets should all be on your packing list[3]. If you like to organize your trip, a travel guide may be helpful. Pack a book, iPad, or other portable leisure things for your own amusement.

Seasonal Clothing

Seasonal climate change in Montreal is quite pronounced. The best times to go sightseeing are often in the spring (mid-April and May) and fall (late September to early November). Therefore, light to medium weight clothing should be sufficient, with a few extra layers for the evenings. In contrast, Montreal's winters may be bitterly cold, so it's important to bring thick winter clothing including coats, hats, scarves, gloves, and boots. Summers can be hot and muggy, so bring a hat for sun protection and lightweight, breathable clothing.

Travel Documents

Your passport is the most important document for foreign travel. You could also need a visa or an Electronic Travel Authorization (ETA) to enter Canada, depending on your nationality. The following items should also be brought: a driver's license (particularly if you intend to rent a car), tickets for your trip or boarding pass, and proof of travel insurance. Additionally, make a note of and carry crucial numbers, such as emergency contact information.

Carry-On

You should pack everything you'll need for the flight and your immediate needs when you arrive in your carry-on bag. It should contain your identification, a means of payment, such as a credit card, and some Canadian currency. Personal goods could include a phone and charger, glasses, sunglasses, or contacts, as well as other personal care items you might require while flying or right away after landing. Think about taking a travel pillow as well for comfort on the plane.

Practical Information

Language and Communication. Despite the fact that the majority of Montrealers speak both French and English, tourists can usually get by with just English. Learning a few fundamental greetings in French can be helpful and appreciated by the locals.

19

Currency and Banking. The Canadian dollar is the official currency (CAD). Although credit and debit cards are generally accepted, it is best to obtain some Canadian currency before departing. In order to avoid any problems with transactions overseas, don't forget to inform your bank of your vacation plans.

Safety. Tourists can feel safe visiting Montreal. However, it's advised to exercise caution, especially in crowded places or at night, as in any big city.

Etiquette. People from Montreal are renowned for their kindness and friendliness. Observe regional traditions and customs, such as the custom of queuing and tipping service providers (usually around 15-20 percent in restaurants).

A visit to Montreal provides a diverse cultural experience that combines the allure of traditional Europe with the energy of contemporary North America. This essay offers a thorough overview of what to pack and useful advice to take into account while organizing your trip to Montreal, ensuring that you are well-equipped to take advantage of everything the city has to offer.

Chapter 2:
Must Visit Places in Montreal

1. Mont-Royal

Mont-Royal, a gorgeous hill that provides breathtaking, expansive views of the entire city and mountains above the south bank, is an emerald treasure located in the center of Montreal. Without climbing the three separate peaks of Mont-Royal, a lush refuge created by none other than the brains behind Central Park in New York City, a trip to Montreal is incomplete. Rise early and take an early-morning hike, stroll, or bus to the summit to escape the crowds of visitors and experience the peace and quiet of the spectacular scenery. Keep in mind that getting up early allows you to see the sunrise and the beautiful, awakened city!

2. Plateau

The eclectic Plateau is our next destination on this journey. This neighborhood is a wonderful fusion of bohemian and bourgeois, with a harmonious blend of calm residential lanes and busy thoroughfares. Find yourself getting lost in the maze-like alleyways lined with colorful rowhouses and spiral staircases as you take in the lively atmosphere of this artistic center. Plateau caters to every taste and inclination with its abundance of offbeat stores, little theaters, comfortable coffee shops, and culinary gems.

3. Old Montreal

Explore Old Montreal, the city's historic district, by meandering through its cobblestone lanes. From its beginnings as a fur trade post in the early 17th century to its current status as a bustling center of activity, this neighborhood is replete with tales of yore.

Here, one can see how the ancient and the new cohabit together; ancient basilicas tower above contemporary skyscrapers, and traditional bistros blend in with cutting-edge cafes. Visit the beautiful Notre-Dame Basilica, explore the fascinating realm of science at the Montreal Science Centre, or take a culinary trip through time at Le Saint-Gabriel.

4. Habitat 67

Habitat 67 is a cutting-edge residential complex that defies accepted principles of urban planning, serving as a tribute to Montreal's talent in the field of architecture. A labyrinthine network of prefabricated concrete forms was created by architect Moshe Safdie for Expo 67, the World's Fair that was hosted in Montreal. It combines practicality and aesthetics. This complicated construction of 146 homes, each with a separate patio, is made up of 354 similar, prefabricated concrete forms joined in different ways.

5. Notre-Dame Basilica of Montreal

The Notre-Dame Basilica, a Gothic Revival architectural gem, must be on your itinerary when visiting Montreal. One of the biggest churches in North America, this enormous structure stands as a testament to Montreal's illustrious past. Admire the beautiful stained glass windows, gilded statues, and detailed woodwork that reflect scenes from the city's religious heritage.

You won't want to miss the captivating light display, which is a tribute to Montreal and its Basilica.

6. Jacques-Cartier Bridge

The Jacques-Cartier Bridge, a five-lane engineering marvel, provides sweeping views of Montreal. It was constructed in 1930 and crosses the Saint Lawrence River to link Montreal with the South Shore of the city. Every night, the bridge dons a brilliant illumination that combines technology and creativity and changes with the seasons and the pulse of the city. The Jacques-Cartier Bridge is an iconic representation of Montreal, whether you're traveling along its lanes on foot, by bicycle, or in a car, or just admiring it from a distance.

7. Underground City

Seize the opportunity to explore the 32-kilometer-long Underground City (RÉSO), a subterranean marvel of Montreal. This labyrinth houses a multitude of establishments - from shops and restaurants to theatres and universities - all interconnected and sheltered from the city's harsh winters. Explore this underground area while taking in the lively atmosphere and wide variety of restaurants and shopping opportunities.

8. The Village

Discover The Village, the welcoming neighborhood that is home to Montreal's LGBTQ+ community and boasts streets that are decked with rainbow flags. It is located along Rue Sainte-Catherine and is teeming with cool bars, chic shops, and cutting-edge galleries. The boulevard becomes a pedestrian-only sanctuary in the summer with patios, outdoor artwork, and live street entertainment. Whether you're an ally or a member of the LGBTQ+ community, you'll always be made to feel welcome at The Village.

9. Olympic Stadium

Visit the famous Olympic Stadium, built for the 1976 Summer Olympics, in Montreal's east end. It stands as a testimony to Montreal's sporting heritage with its distinctive inclined tower, the tallest of its kind in the world. Nowadays, a wide variety of sporting events, concerts, and trade exhibits are held at the Stadium.

10. Biodome

The Biodome, a magnificent exhibit of our planet's varied ecosystems, is located just next to the Olympic Stadium. An immersive ecological experience has been created in the Biodome, formerly an Olympic velodrome. You can travel from the lush rainforests of South America to the subpolar regions of the Atlantic by walking through recreations of the four most magnificent ecosystems in the Americas.

11. Place Ville Marie

Place Ville Marie is a prominent cruciform skyscraper that stands as a tribute to the development of the city and serves as a landmark of Montreal's downtown skyline. From its observatory at the top, you can take in 360-degree views of Montreal. A sizable underground shopping center offers a wide variety of food and retail alternatives below.

12. Parc Jean-Drapeau

Parc Jean-Drapeau, which located in the middle of the Saint Lawrence River, is a haven for outdoor pursuits. It is made up of Saint Helen's Island and artificial Notre Dame Island and offers a variety of activities, from peaceful picnic areas and relaxing beachfront to an amusement park and the yearly Osheaga music festival.

13. Montreal Casino

Visit Canada's largest casino, Montreal Casino, and try your luck. The casino offers a wide range of entertainment options in addition to its gaming tables and slot machines, including performances, restaurants, bars, and occasionally even fireworks.

14. Marché Jean-Talon

At Marché Jean-Talon, one of the biggest open-air marketplaces in North America, indulge your taste buds with the delectable flavors of Quebec. Fresh fruits, vegetables, cheeses, bread, pastries, and a plethora of high-quality regional goods are available here from local producers and artisans.

15. Quartier des Spectacles / Place des Festivals

Enter Montreal's thriving Quartier des Spectacles, the city's cultural center. It holds more than a hundred events each year and has more than 30 performing spaces, including the Place des

Festivals. In this thriving area, there is always a spectacle to enjoy, whether it be in the form of movies, music, theater, or dance.

16. Canadian Centre for Architecture

The Canadian Centre for Architecture is a global research organization that operates under the guiding principle that architecture is a matter of public interest. The CCA promotes a deeper knowledge and study of architecture's role in society through its exhibitions, research, public activities, and collection of architectural archives.

17. Notre-Dame-de-Bon-Secours Chapel

The Notre-Dame-de-Bon-Secours Chapel, often called the Sailor's Church, is one of Montreal's oldest chapels. This ancient treasure, decorated with ex-votos with maritime themes, provides a peaceful sanctuary away from the bustle of the city.

18. Chinatown

Experience Montreal's Chinatown's lively sights, sounds, and flavors firsthand. It's a mash-up of Asian culture and cuisine, with classic tea houses alongside Cantonese dim lunch, bubble tea businesses, and Asian bakeries.

19. Botanical Gardens

Spend the day in Montreal's Botanical Gardens, one of the biggest in the world, a lush paradise. Its 190 acres include 10 exhibition greenhouses and themed gardens. The Gardens guarantee a lovely refuge, whether it is the calm of the Japanese Garden or the vibrancy of the Tropical Rainforest that appeals.

20. L'Oratoire Saint-Joseph

Admire the magnificent L'Oratoire Saint-Joseph, Canada's biggest church, which has a commanding position atop Westmount Summit and provides panoramic views of the city. Discover its enormous Renaissance-style dome, stunning chapel, and lush gardens.

21. Montreal Metro

Discover the Montreal Metro, a crucial aspect of the city's ambiance. This large subway system is renowned for its distinctive public art and architecture, and each station has a unique look and feel. A metro ride is more than just a means of transportation; it is also a cultural event.

22. La Ronde

La Ronde, Quebec's biggest theme park, is the perfect place to let your adventurous side loose. A day of family-friendly entertainment is guaranteed at this Six Flags property, which features a variety of roller coasters, activities, performances, and fireworks.

23. Schwartz's

Enjoy the finest smoked pork in Montreal at Schwartz's, a hallmark of the city's culinary scene since 1928. This historic deli, located in the trendy Plateau neighborhood, provides a typical Montreal dining experience.

24. Parc La Fontaine

Relax in the beautiful surroundings of Parc La Fontaine, a peaceful haven in the heart of the city. It is the ideal location for leisurely strolls, picnics, or just reading a book because of its lovely ponds, trees, and art works.

25. Lachine Canal

Finally, go for a leisurely stroll or a picturesque bike ride along the Lachine Canal. It's 14.5 km long and offers breathtaking views of the city as well as the former factories that formerly lined Montreal's industrial district. Its banks are bustling with locals and visitors alike throughout the summer as they engage in water sports, picnics, and barbecues.

The vibrant city of Montreal provides a wide range of experiences that fascinate the senses. It is a must-visit location for both tourists and locals due to its interesting blend of old-world elegance and modern dynamism, cultural richness and gastronomic delights, green parks, and trendy neighborhoods.

Chapter 3:
Itineraries

With their distinctive fusion of history, culture, food, and adventure, Montreal and Quebec, two bustling cities tucked away in the heart of French Canada, lure curious visitors. This travel guide aims to capture the essence of these global gems by providing a diverse schedule that makes it easy for you to travel across their charming neighborhoods and exciting cities.

The Five-Day Exploration Itinerary

Day 1 – The Historical Heart of Montreal

Start your adventure in Old Montreal, the city's historic area. To gain a thorough appreciation of the city's history, take a guided walking tour of the cobblestone streets. After indulging your senses with Montreal's past, indulge your palate at Taverne Gaspar, a former warehouse that has been transformed into a restaurant. Here, you can savor pub fare with a French influence. Don't forget to visit Montreal Poutine to satisfy your craving for the renowned Quebecois cuisine, poutine.

Day 2 – The Cultural Landscape of Montreal

Visit the Pointe-à-Callière Museum of Archaeology and History to delve further into Montreal's cultural foundations. At the site where the city was built, immerse yourself in its past. After your encounter with history, relax at the Bota Bota spa, which offers a variety of calming treatments and looks out over the picturesque Old Port.

Day 3 – Montreal Nightlife

The city of Montreal starts to really shine as the sun sets. Enjoy your meal at Modavie, a jazz bar and restaurant on Saint-Paul Street, while experiencing the lively local music. Visit the Coldroom to end your day; it's a hidden gem with a prohibition-era atmosphere that gives your evening a dash of adventure.

Day 4 – En Route to Quebec City

Take the scenic Corridor Service train from VIA Rail to Quebec City for your trip. With its blend of historical sites and vivacious nightlife, the city's European flair is certain to capture your attention.

Day 5 – Historic Wonders of Quebec City

On a narrated walking tour, learn the core of Quebec City's history. Discover the Basilica, the Place Royale, and the Latin Quarter, each of which exudes a distinct charm. As you stroll through the cobblestone streets, take in the city's unique fusion of modernity and history.

The One-Week Itinerary

The five days of exploration listed above are included in the one-week program, along with two additional days filled with excitement.

Day 6 – The Gastronomic Delights of Quebec City

The cuisine scene in Quebec City is vibrant and diverse, offering food lovers a wide range of gourmet delights. Take a culinary tour of the city and sample regional specialties and foreign cuisines at the lively markets and charming eateries.

Day 7 – Winter Adventures in Quebec City

Visit Hotel De Glace, North America's only ice hotel, during the winter if you're in town during the colder months. The Winter Carnival, which is Quebec's favorite cold-weather activity, offers a distinctive cultural encounter.

The Weekend Getaway

Day 1 – Montreal's Cultural Landscape

Take a tour of Old Montreal and the Pointe-à-Callière Museum to get your adventure started. Enjoy the delicious food at Taverne Gaspar and Montreal Poutine to give your exploration a tasty start. Enjoy Bota Bota spa's soothing services to cap off the day.

Day 2 – The Historical Charm of Quebec City

Take the Corridor Service train from VIA Rail to Quebec City. Take a walking tour to start off your trip and learn about the city's architectural wonders and historical monuments. At one of the city's thriving food markets, you may round out your day by sampling regional specialties.

These itineraries guarantee an immersive experience, giving you a taste of Montreal and Quebec City's historical beauty, cultural richness, and culinary delights, regardless of how long you visit.

Chapter 4: Best Restaurants and Cuisine in Montreal

For food lovers, Montreal is like a tapestry made of various culinary threads. The vivacious Quebec city is filled to the brim with a cornucopia of dining establishments, each of which exudes a special character and a palate of flavors from around the world. The 38 top Montreal restaurants that rule the culinary landscape are examined in-depth in this article.

Île Flottante

Île Flottante is a hidden gem that promotes seasonal and local produce combined with French skills. It is located in Montreal's hip Mile End. Its gastronomic offerings feature a medley of flavors that honor Montreal's rich natural richness and cultural diversity.

Vin Mon Lapin

Vin Mon Lapin is a gastronomic sanctuary where innovative meals are paired with an exceptional assortment of natural wines. Known for its friendly ambiance, this restaurant provides a unique eating experience with its selection of interesting tapas.

Mousso

The tasting menu at Chef Antonin Mousseau-Mousso Rivard's is seasonal, and it is the pinnacle of culinary talent. This eatery, which exudes a simple elegance, seduces customers with its mouthwatering and cutting-edge dishes.

Toqué!

Toqué! is a symbol of gourmet cuisine and the city's French heritage. This restaurant, promoted by Chef Normand Laprise, uses regional ingredients from Quebec to create dishes that are both aesthetically beautiful and delectable.

Okeya Kyujiro

In the heart of Montreal, Okeya Kyujiro offers a genuine Japanese culinary experience. The restaurant serves a broad range of

Japanese cuisine, from precisely prepared sushi to umami-rich ramen.

Maison Boulud

Under the culinary guidance of renowned chef Daniel Boulud and located inside the magnificent Ritz-Carlton, Maison Boulud presents diners to a refined rendition of traditional French cuisine. The excellent ambiance of the restaurant is complemented by the painstakingly designed food.

Park

Park offers a menu infused with Korean and Japanese flavors and is synonymous with elevated sushi experiences. The culinary works of chef Antonio Park represent a transcendental gourmet trip and are a testament to sustainability and seasonality.

Moccione

The Moccione restaurant is a model of Italian cuisine. The pasta expert adds a modern twist to classic dishes to give them new life. The cozy environment enhances the allure of the culinary story.

Joe Beef

Joe Beef is renowned for its menu that focuses heavily on meat. This restaurant celebrates extravagance and brings a hint of rustic charm to the Montreal dining scene. It is well known for their lavish lobster pasta and extensive wine selection.

Mastard

With an emphasis on the history and cuisine of Quebec, Mastard, run by famous chef Simon Mathys, carves out a distinctive niche. Diners may enjoy the gastronomic adventure of the province thanks to the menu's constant evolution and reliance on regional ingredients.

Hoogan et Beaufort

Hoogan et Beaufort pays a magnificent homage to the terroir of Quebec by masterfully fusing traditional cooking methods with cutting-edge culinary sensibility. Their method of cooking over an open fire penetrates the entire menu, providing an exceptional gastronomic experience.

Bouillon Bilk

Bouillon Bilk offers refined cuisine that are a treat for the senses in a minimalist setting. The restaurant's creative menu, complemented by beautiful presentation, establishes it as a major participant in the city's culinary scene.

Vin Papillon

Vin Papillon provides a unique dining experience by embracing a menu that emphasizes vegetables. This Joe Beef-affiliated restaurant supports regional ingredients with creative cuisine and a wide variety of natural wines.

La Chronique

To avoid repetition, a center of good dining. La Franquette Bistro

Bistro La Franquette is a steadfast landmark in the city's culinary scene, welcoming customers with a beautiful fusion of French provincial charm and modern Montreal flair. The restaurant specializes in traditional French fare that has been given a distinctively Quebecois flavor. Along with a large wine list that features an outstanding selection from the renowned vineyards of Bordeaux and Champagne, the strong tastes of Coq au Vin and Ratatouille transport customers to the culinary heart of France.

Chez Sophie

Enjoy the lively atmosphere at Chez Sophie, where French and Mediterranean food meld beautifully. Enjoy the fresh seafood-topped house-made pasta or the restaurant's signature roast lamb shank, which smoothly slips off the bone. The appeal of Chez Sophie also extends to its appearance. Your dining experience will be made more romantic by the breathtaking views of the St. Lawrence River from the floor to ceiling windows.

Time Out Market Montreal

The Time Out Market Montreal, a true gastronomic hotspot, is a culinary feast that satisfies all cravings under one roof. This food hall, which has several renowned local eateries, enables customers to enjoy a variety of cuisines, from Middle Eastern to Vietnamese. Enjoy the variety of scents in the air as you revel in a new flavor at each turn. The relaxed seating encourages a lively, communal dining experience, creating a friendly environment for customers.

Tunnel Espresso

Tunnel Espresso is a secret gem for coffee lovers, brewing with dedication. The espresso, made expertly by trained baristas into a heavenly shot of crema-laden perfection, is the café's specialty. French pastries and espresso make an easy yet delightful pick-me-up.

Le Blossom

Le Blossom is renowned for its breathtaking cherry blossom tree interior, but its fascination extends beyond the surface. The restaurant offers mouthwatering hand-rolled sushi, alluring sashimi, and a variety of mouthwatering Japanese specialties. The sake menu is broad and offers wonderful variations of the rice wine to match your sushi properly.

Marusan

Japanese comfort food lovers will find Marusan to be a refuge, offering a cozy eating experience. The menu is brief and focuses on tonkatsu, udon noodles, and other classic foods. Each is made with the utmost care, producing flavors that are both genuine and enduring.

Le Red Tiger

Le Red Tiger offers a bold dive into Vietnamese street food and is brimming with a vibrant energy. The menu is filled with vibrant, shareable delicacies including papaya salad, pho soups, and lemongrass chicken. Every dish showcases Vietnam's vibrant culture within the busy environment.

Le Taj

At Le Taj, immerse yourself in the savory, spicy world of Indian cuisine. This restaurant offers a selection of Indian staples like butter chicken, tandoori delicacies, and a range of mouthwatering naan bread, all of which are served from a menu rooted in centuries-old customs. The handcrafted architectural details in the inside, which are reminiscent of opulent Indian palaces, provide a magical eating environment.

Paul Toussaint

Chef Paul Toussaint is in charge of this thriving Caribbean restaurant and is constructing a tropical getaway right in the middle of Montreal. The meals include tastes from Trinidad,

Jamaica, and Haiti. Jerk chicken, griot (Haitian-style pork), and accra are examples of signature dishes (Caribbean fritters). A sip of one of their rum-based cocktails whisks you away to Caribbean beaches that are bathed in sunlight.

Americas BBQ

Americas BBQ offers a filling menu as a celebration of smokey, succulent, and flavorful barbecue cuisine. to proceed to the next.

Chapter 5:
Accommodations in Montreal

The city of Montreal, which is frequently referred to as Canada's "European" city, is enticing because it combines charm, history, and a distinctive cultural experience. Montreal, the historic capital of Canada and one of the five major French-speaking cities in the world, distinguishes out from the competition because to its unique personality and energetic atmosphere. Montreal provides a variety of outstanding options for travelers looking for lodging that captures the charm of the city and ensures comfort during their stay. In this post, we'll examine some of Montreal's best tourist-friendly lodging options, displaying its amenities and features.

1. Hotel Nelligan

Hotel Nelligan, located in the center of Old Montreal, offers a mesmerizing fusion of antiquity and contemporary elegance. With its exposed brick walls and modern furnishings, this boutique hotel exudes a warm and welcoming ambiance. The hotel offers guests opulent rooms and suites that offer a cozy and fashionable refuge. With its excellent location, visitors can easily explore Old Montreal's cobblestone streets, go to neighboring museums and art galleries, and revel in the city's thriving culinary scene.

2. Sonder Maisonneuve

In the heart of Montreal's bustling downtown, Sonder Maisonneuve offers completely furnished apartments for a distinctive lodging experience. With contemporary conveniences and thoughtful touches, these chic apartments are made to make visitors feel at home. Whether guests are lone explorers or families visiting the city, Sonder Maisonneuve offers a range of accommodations from studios to multi-bedroom apartments to suit their needs. The hotel's convenient location makes it simple to get to well-liked sights, retail areas, and a variety of food selections.

3. Hotel Place d'Armes Old Montreal

The Hotel Place d'Armes Old Montreal is the perfect option for travelers looking for opulence and history. In addition to showcasing the city's rich architectural legacy, this elegant hotel provides guests with a calm hideaway in the center of Old Montreal. The luxuriously furnished rooms and suites offer contemporary amenities and a calm atmosphere. Due to its close proximity to famous sites like Notre-Dame Basilica and the Vieux Séminaire de St-Sulpice, visitors may fully experience the area's medieval charm.

4. Le Mount Stephen

In the heart of Montreal, Le Mount Stephen provides a refined and opulent lodging experience. This boutique hotel, housed in a lovingly renovated estate, skillfully blends old-world elegance with contemporary conveniences. The elegantly decorated rooms and suites provide expansive views of the city. The hotel's restaurant offers fine dining, and its rooftop patio offers stunning views of the neighborhood cityscape while guests unwind with a drink.

5. Hotel William Gray

Hotel William Gray, located in the center of Old Montreal, combines modern architecture with a dash of the past. This boutique hotel offers chic guestrooms and suites with contemporary conveniences that give a peaceful retreat from the busy metropolis. Visitors can take in expansive views of the Old Port and the St. Lawrence River from the rooftop deck. The hotel's ideal location makes it simple to reach well-known landmarks, beautiful cafés, and chic stores.

6. Le Saint-Sulpice

A tranquil and private retreat is available at Le Saint-Sulpice in the heart of Old Montreal. This all-suite hotel offers roomy, exquisitely furnished lodgings with a separate living space and a fully functional kitchenette. The hotel's inviting garden is a great place to unwind, and the on-site restaurant serves French-inspired fare. The hotel is a great option for travellers because of its close proximity to sights including Place Jacques-Cartier and the Montreal Museum of Archaeology and History.

7. Auberge du Vieux-Port

For visitors to Montreal, Auberge du Vieux-Port provides a charming and romantic location in a historic structure with views of the St. Lawrence River. The boutique hotel offers tastefully decorated rooms and suites, each of which is specially created to highlight the history of the structure. The hotel's renowned restaurant serves up delectable French fare, and guests can also unwind with a cocktail on the rooftop terrace while admiring the city skyline and river views.

8. Hotel Bonaventure Montreal

With its beautiful rooftop garden and outdoor pool, Hotel Bonaventure Montreal offers a distinctive lodging experience, creating a calm haven in the middle of downtown Montreal. Modern facilities and expansive city views are included in the room sizes and comfort levels of the suites and rooms. Visitors can repose in the spa at the hotel, eat at the restaurant there, or visit the nearby cultural centers and shopping centers.

9. DoubleTree by Hilton Montreal

The DoubleTree by Hilton Montreal offers modern accommodations and top-notch service in the thriving Quartier des Spectacles. Tourists can unwind in the hotel's beautiful rooms and suites, which come with contemporary conveniences. Visitors can enjoy a delectable dinner at the property's restaurant, unwind on the rooftop terrace, or explore the neighboring theaters and entertainment hotspots that make this part of Montreal so vibrant.

10. Le Square Phillips Hotel & Suites

For visitors to Montreal, the Le Square Phillips Hotel & Rooms offers large, luxurious suites that act as a home away from home. The apartments' fully functional kitchens, distinct living spaces, and contemporary amenities provide for a relaxing and practical stay. The hotel's rooftop patio, fitness facility, and complimentary breakfast are all available to guests. The hotel's convenient location makes it simple to visit well-known landmarks, retail areas, and restaurants.

To meet the interests and tastes of travelers to this intriguing city, Montreal has a wide variety of lodging options. Each lodging offers a distinctive experience, from modern apartments to boutique hotels steeped in history. These lodgings offer the ideal starting point for an enjoyable trip to Montreal, whether visitors opt to savor Old Montreal's beauty or discover the bustling downtown region.

Chapter 6: Romantic Things to do in Montreal

Finding the ideal location for dating can occasionally be a hassle. Such pressure is present. The location should be enjoyable and have the right atmosphere to start a conversation, but it should also light a fire within of you. It can also impair your ability to make decisions, which is made worse if you are unfamiliar with the surroundings. Do not worry, as Canada beckons you to her romantic place in the Quebec province, be it impressing your partner or spicing things up, Montreal is the city you need to be in.

Time to Get Romantic

At the adorable tiny eatery The Triple Crown Dinette in Little Italy, treat your lover to the best Southern comfort food in Montreal. You get everything: collard greens, sweet potatoes, and mac and cheese. You can also take a picnic basket that has already been filled from the restaurant and go to the Little Italy Park next to it. A delicious and romantic picnic in the park! Isn't this a timeless date? You don't need to cook because you have someone else take care of it. All you have to do is savor the delectable fare and take in each other's romanticism. With the assistance of these hip eateries, you may make your evening extra unforgettable.

How romantic would it be to take a lengthy stroll by the river on a date? Walking beside the river in the Lachine Canal is really tranquil. You can start at the Atwater market, pick up a wonderful pizza or some seasonal fruit, and then walk with your spouse toward Old Montreal while holding hands. Do you desire more intrigue on the date? There you can rent a bike and ride alongside your lover while enjoying the wind in your face and the movement of her lovely hair. Rent a boat or kayak, perhaps a tandem kayak if you want to make things more romantic, and start engaging in exciting water races.

Make your lover feel like a princess or a prince, do you want to? Therefore, a high tea at Roselys, the restaurant in the Queen Elizabeth hotel, will surprise them. The greatest tea, scones, bite-sized sandwiches (three-tier variety), and delicious sweet delights are all included for $37. The menu will be detailed in great length, and reading it will teach you something.

So, if tea isn't your cup of tea, head to the speakeasies! There are a number of secret speakeasies in Montreal, but you should know where to look. Once you and your companion have entered the underground, you will both begin to become more daring as you realize that you have discovered something together. If you are a solitary traveler visiting the city, you can also take a tinder date to the bar and make an effort to impress her there! You'll be encouraged by the setting to relax and get to know your date, and vice versa.

A visit to a museum may make for an incredible romantic date, and Montreal is brimming with museums! They are world-famous museums with an astounding number of exhibits, not just any old museums. You may even check out the nearby galleries, as they frequently host amazing exhibits and events. You will learn something new about one another as a result of the tour, not just in the museum but also about yourselves!

Movie and Wine

The ideal date is always watching a movie together! Consider seeing it in IMAX 3D. awesome, no? Your mind will be blown by the selection that the Montreal Science Center makes for its theater performances. They had demonstrations on how to make your own movie and how to make movies. The interactive and cool multimedia approach employed in the exhibitions will have you playing and laughing, so you and your spouse will both enjoy the show. What a fantastic date it would be if it could make both of you feel like kids again! The website montrealsciencecentre.com has all the information you need.

After a long day of exploration, how about unwinding with a dinner and some cold beverages? The ideal setting for getting to know one another is over a delectable meal and enticing beverage! The facility is indeed ready! Darling may provide you a great romantic twilight without making your wallet light. A café by day and a bustling tiny bar by night. The drink energizes the atmosphere, which is set by the lighting's alluring amber hue. The great Canadian singer-songwriter Leonard Cohen, one of the biggest loves the city has ever produced, lived across the street from this incredibly stylish bar-café. Isn't this sufficient to give you the impression that you are the ultimate lover? Visit Instagram to learn more about the bar at bar.darling.

Without wine, what would romance be? Wouldn't it be fantastic to sit next to your significant other and watch him or her enjoy the delicious wine while casting enticing glances your way? Visit the Rouge Gorge to see what a wine bar is all about! It's the ideal romantic setting to spend an evening as you prepare to unwind with a bottle of wine because the serene and cool atmosphere makes you feel warm. The establishment stays open until 2 AM. Although there is no obligation to order food, the kitchen does offer little bits if you are hungry. Don't hold back when the wine starts to take effect and you feel the want to burst into song and dance. Visit their speakeasy, Le Royal, downstairs! For further details, go to rougegorge.ca on their website.

Are you preparing to merge with nature so that you and your spouse can experience the airy love? You won't be disappointed with Montreal! You may connect with nature at The Kabin's Sutton Resort, which provides a 360-degree view of the surrounding lovely woodland. Depending on the season, you may add a little adventure by going skiing at the adjacent hill or going on a romantic trek to a waterfall. The resort has a cottage with a personal hot tub that makes for the ideal luxurious getaway. You may also utilize their kitchen and cook there, and this service is offered all year long. You and your spouse can go exploring in the surrounding town!

Romantic Things to do in Quebec City

One of the most romantic towns in the world and a favourite honeymoon destination, Quebec City is alive, beautiful, and charismatic. The city's European design makes it the ideal fantasy setting for lovers to experience their love and take in the atmosphere. The best honeymoon memories can be created while holding hands and strolling through streets adorned with European-style architecture, sneaking a kiss in a busy amusement park, and having a romantic supper in a restaurant with low lighting.

Take a ride on the well-known Hop on Hop off bus tour of the city if you're seeking for an exciting, enjoyable vacation with your special someone. Sit atop a double-decker bus and gaze out over Quebec City while placing your hands on your partner's shoulder. At each of the twelve stops the bus will make, you may learn more about this historic city. Enjoy the renowned Notre-Dame-des-Victoires and the Quebec Citadel as well. The best place to reignite the flame of love and create enduring memories is Old Quebec, a UNESCO World Heritage site.

Feel the Love

Learn about Mayan chocolate, its roots, and how they helped spread chocolate over the world by visiting the cutting-edge Erico Chocolate Museum and Chocolate Shop. It also contains over 200 items from the Caribbean Islands, Europe, and Mexico. Warm up with a nice cup of hot chocolate and some treats from their shop.

Experience authentic French food while dining by candlelight in an Old Quebec restaurant. Get a bottle of wine and something delicious to finish your dinner. Take your lover for a stroll through the neighborhood streets to admire the spectacular city lights.

The St. Lawrence River may be seen in breathtaking beauty from the famous Chateau Frontenac. Without spending money on a hotel stay, you can experience the romantic ambiance at the 1608 Wine & Cheese bar. Take in the splendor of the river's natural beauty as you savor a delicious dinner. Take a tour to see the Fairmont Le Chateau Frontenac up close.

Quebec City has the best morning food in the world. The wide variety of cafes and restaurants available will make it simple for you to satisfy your morning hunger desires. While sipping a cappuccino and watching Quebec City awaken, indulge in a plate of delicious crepes!

Image Source: Pixabay

You and your spouse can take a stroll through the neighborhood's winding cobblestone lanes and prepare to be astounded by the historic buildings. The little bistros and modest shops that line the streets make up one of the city's best romantic areas.

The Observatoire de la Capitale, an observation deck, is located on the 31st level of the Marie-Guyart building and offers a complete 360-degree view of the city. As you and your spouse take in the beauty of the city from a height of 221 meters, get ready to witness the majesty of nature.

Would you like to celebrate Quebec's rural customs with your better half? Visit the Ile d'Orleans, which is five kilometers east of the city center in the St. Lawrence River. You can visit a farm and engage in some farmer's market shopping. The region brings back New France's vibrant and diverse culture. As you float around the river, observe the city's sunset panorama.

Don't let the splendor of Montmorency Falls pass you by; take a pleasant half-day excursion to the Falls and Ste-Anne-de-Beaupre. An endearing way to your city tour!

Interesting Getaways Based On Your Budget

Quebec City is a romantic city even without Valentine's Day, a lovely bunch of flowers, or the eye-catching red hearts. These three getaways are affordable for all budget sizes, making them ideal for romantic getaways.

Get Posh

Do you want to truly make your partner feel like a princess? She must be brought to the Auberge Saint-Antoine. This first-rate boutique hotel features an attractive model and a novel take on contemporary luxury. It resembles a royal palace because to the spectacular new-style decor and priceless New France relics.

When you enter the Panorama Suite, you are greeted with specially imported champagne and your fantasy trip starts. You both feel like a royal pair thanks to the chic, shiny furnishings, the elegant marble shower, and the breathtaking view of the frozen river. While being hugged by the warmth of a central fireplace, the gourmet dining area features a combination of intriguing contemporary concepts and the aged beams of a vintage maritime warehouse.

Try the chefs' distinctive dishes, such as Paris-Brest-Quebec (a rich but delicate pouf of cider-glazed apples, pecan praline, shortbread, and maple mousse), to get a taste of their culinary appeal.

Not-so-costly romance

One of the tiniest hotels in Quebec City, Hotel Le Priori is a chic boutique establishment in Old Quebec that dates back to 1734. Along with its modern urban furnishings, it also has a trendy café under the name of Toast. Their top-tier Clefs d'Or concierge may arrange for you to go on ski trips, go sightseeing, and visit museums.

As you explore the room, you'll be surprised by the white-draped beds, the old stone and brick walls, iPod docs, glass showers, flat TVs, etc. The romantic room, No. 401, at the hotel, which includes 28 suites and rooms with enticing hideaways, is the best. It is a two-level junior suite with a queen bed, a working fireplace, a kitchenette, and a private outdoor whirlpool tub on the balcony.

One of the thriving restaurants in the Old City that specialized in French-style cuisine is the trendy Restaurant Toast. Couples can have a romantic meal here because of the quaint setting and stone walls.

Exceptionally big for a small pocket

If your bank account doesn't support your huge heart, the effective and contemporary HI-Auberge Internationale de Québec will function nicely for you. The hotel is located in Upper Town, halfway between Hotel du Parlement and Chateau Frontenac, in the heart of three ancient structures. The motel has sixteen individual rooms and is arranged and modern.

You can turn the private retreat in the 1789 French Revolution-era home into personal snuggle bed! historical, romantic, and budget-friendly! If you're a solo traveler and would like some company, the hotel chain's activities schedule will guarantee that you're never alone!

In their hostel part, they also feature a fantastic bar, a shared kitchen, a TV lounge, and 29 dorm rooms. Prepare to participate in free guided tours, bar crawls, bus excursions to Montmorency Falls, boat rides to Levis, and ice skating. Le Bureau de Poste, a rustic bistro in the hip St. Roch neighborhood, serves delicious meals for $5, including spicy Asian cuisine.

Chapter 7:
Cultural Activities in Montreal

The bustling metropolis of Greater Montréal, Montreal, is well known for its wide range of cultural influences and burgeoning arts community. Due to its size and the wide variety of cultural activities it provides, this cosmopolitan metropolis stands out among urban centers in North America [1]. Greater Montréal offers a wide range of alternatives for both residents and visitors, including festivals, exhibitions, museums, concerts, and performances, thanks to its multicultural makeup. This article delves into the relevance of cultural events in the city and highlights its cultural vibrancy to examine why Greater Montréal is a cultural hub.

Major Festivals in Greater Montréal

The International Jazz Festival

A major event on Montreal's cultural calendar, the International Jazz Festival draws well-known jazz musicians from all over the world. This yearly occasion enthralls music lovers with its thrilling performances and revitalizes the city.

FrancoFolies

FrancoFolies honors the French-speaking music community and presents the abilities of both domestic and foreign francophone performers. It serves as a stage for a variety of musical genres, encouraging cross-cultural interaction and creative expression.

Piknic Électronik

Summertime brings about the distinctive outdoor electronic music festival known as Piknic Électronik. It gives music lovers an amazing experience by fusing electronic sounds with beautiful scenery.

Montréal en Lumière

During the winter, Montréal en Lumière lights up the city, mesmerizing both residents and tourists with its eye-catching light works, creative events, and culinary treats.

Igloofest

Igloofest is an outdoor electronic music festival that celebrates the essence of winter. Dancers brave the chilly weather to groove to popular DJs' sounds, providing a thrilling experience beneath the winter sky.

Osheaga

The well-known music event Osheaga features a diverse range of performers, from rock and pop to indie and alternative. It draws fans of music from all over, adding to the city's thriving music scene.

Just for Laughs Comedy Festival

Top comics from across the world perform at the Just for Laughs Comedy Festival, which brings joy and laughter to Montreal. It is a celebration of comedy and provides a stage for both well-known and up-and-coming comedians.

Festival du Nouveau Cinéma

The Festival du Nouveau Cinéma showcases cutting-edge, original films in a variety of disciplines. It offers a forum for upcoming filmmakers and presents films that provoke discussion and challenge accepted narrative conventions.

ZooFest

An annual event called ZooFest features a wide variety of performing arts, such as comedy, music, theater, and more. It acts as a stage for up-and-coming performers, giving them a chance to display their abilities.

Cultural Events All Year Round

Exhibitions and art shows

Numerous exhibitions and art shows with regional and international artists are held annually in Greater Montréal. These occasions give art lovers the chance to discover various artistic mediums and interact with stimulating visual experiences.

Concerts and performances

All throughout the year, a variety of musical preferences are catered to via concerts and shows. The city offers a wide variety of acts that enthrall people, from classical symphonies to modern concerts.

Theatre programming

Montreal's theater scene is thriving, with a wide array of productions ranging from classical plays to avant-garde performances. Theaters in the city offer a stage for regional and international performers, resulting in a varied and exciting theatrical experience.

Local and international productions

Greater Montréal acts as a focal point for both national and international shows, drawing renowned creatives like musicians, actors, and musicians. This influx of talent boosts the city's cultural life and creates opportunities for cross-cultural interaction.

Cultural Venues in Greater Montréal

Performance venues

1. Overview of downtown performance venues

Over 180 performance venues can be found in the downtown region of Greater Montréal, all of which contribute to the city's thriving cultural scene. These locations offer a wide variety of creative experiences, from small theaters to large concert halls.

2. Place des Arts complex

Six concert and theater facilities at the Place des Arts complex serve as the city's cultural hub and stage a range of shows. This legendary location presents a wide variety of cultural undertakings, from ballet and opera to plays and musical events.

3. Quartier des Spectacles

The Quartier des Spectacles, a bustling neighborhood next to Place des Arts, is well-known for its active cultural scene. It acts as a focal point for festivals, outdoor events, and artistic projects, giving both tourists and residents an immersive experience.

Museums and art galleries

1. Overview of museums in the city

The Greater Montréal region is home to a wide variety of museums and art galleries. These organizations offer a window into the cultural heritage of the city and various aesthetic expressions from throughout the world, ranging from modern art to historical antiques.

2. Musée d'art contemporain

A well-known cultural institution, the Musée d'art contemporain (Museum of Contemporary Art) exhibits contemporary works of art by national and international artists. It provides exhibitions that provoke thought and promotes discussion of current artistic techniques.

3. Other notable museums and galleries

Greater Montréal is home to various more renowned museums and art galleries in addition to the Musée d'art contemporain. These organizations, like the McCord Museum, the Canadian Centre for Architecture, and the Montreal Museum of Fine Arts, enrich the city's cultural fabric by preserving and showcasing priceless works of art.

Cultural Communities in Greater Montréal

Overview of cultural communities

Over 120 different cultural groups from five continents are represented in the Greater Montréal area [3]. The social fabric of the city is enriched by this ethnic tapestry, which also strengthens its sense of individuality.

Importance of multiculturalism

Greater Montréal's multicultural communities stimulate intercultural discussion, promote diversity and inclusivity, and cultivate mutual understanding. It increases the cultural vibrancy of the city and broadens perspectives and horizons.

Impact on local culture and identity

Cultural communities have a significant influence on Greater Montréal's local culture and identity. They contribute to the city's cuisine, customs, celebrations, and artistic expressions, fostering a dynamic and vibrant cultural environment that embodies the inclusive nature of the community.

Privileged Access Programs

Accès Montréal Card

Montrealers can benefit from a variety of perks, including discounts, special offers, and competitions, with the Accès Montréal Card. It acts as a starting point for more convenient and economical access to the city's cultural attractions.

Passeport MTL étudiant international

The Passeport MTL étudiant international is designed specifically for newly arrived international students, providing them with privileged access to cultural events, special offers, and networking activities. Its goal is to better integrate them into Greater Montréal's cultural landscape.

Passeport MTL culture

Tourists have access to the vibrant cultural offerings of the city thanks to Tourisme Montréal's Passeport MTL culture. It allows tourists to easily enjoy the city's great variety of cultural activities by providing free public transportation for 24 or 72 hours.

Avantages Laval Card

Residents of Laval, a city in the Greater Montréal area, get access to special advantages and savings on cultural events with the Avantages Laval Card. It motivates locals to take part in the cultural scene and discover what their neighborhood has to offer.

Accès Longueuil Card

Residents of Longueuil, a different Greater Montréal suburb, have preferential access to cultural events and attractions thanks to the Accès Longueuil Card. It aims to enhance people of Longueuil's cultural experiences and promote a sense of community involvement.

Cultural Offerings in Suburban Areas

Laval

Laval, a thriving suburb of Greater Montréal, provides a variety of cultural pursuits. It offers a specialized cultural experience by hosting festivals, exhibits, and performances that are tailored to the preferences of its citizens.

Longueuil

Another Greater Montréal suburb, Longueuil, offers a wide variety of cultural options. Longueuil offers its citizens opportunities to interact with the local arts and culture scene through community activities and art exhibitions.

Greater Montréal's Global Connections

Influence of immigrants from around the world

Immigrants who have chosen to make Greater Montréal their home come from a variety of origins, which has a significant impact on the city's multiculturalism. Their presence has enriched the cultural environment and helped to build a global metropolis that welcomes all cultures, languages, and viewpoints.

Culinary diversity and international cuisine

Greater Montréal's culinary sector reflects the city's connections to the world. A broad variety of international cuisines are available at restaurants, cafes, and food markets, enabling locals and guests to travel the world through food without ever leaving the city.

Cultural festivals representing different cultures

Cultural celebrations honoring particular communities, such the Festival du monde arabe and the Festival international Nuits d'Afrique, offer venues for artistic expression and highlight various regions' rich cultural legacies. Through the presentation of music, dance, and visual arts, these festivals promote appreciation for and understanding of many cultures.

The function of media in fostering ties with home countries

Greater Montréal inhabitants keep in touch with their home nations via a variety of media outlets, including television, radio, and the internet. These media outlets bridge the gap between home countries and the city's diverse culture by acting as platforms for news, entertainment, and cultural material.

Greater Montréal is recognized as a significant cultural hub due to its multiculturalism and thriving arts scene. Major festivals, year-round cultural events, and a variety of venues all add to the city's appeal. Greater Montréal's cultural diversity is further boosted by the presence of multicultural populations, special access programs, suburban cultural activities, and international linkages. Both tourists and locals are encouraged to experience the city's numerous creative offerings, immerse themselves in its vibrant cultural offerings, and embrace the distinctive cultural tapestry that characterizes this global metropolis.

Chapter 8: Nightlife And Festivals In Montreal

Most people are aware of the exciting nightlife that Montreal has to offer. However, the advertisements and talking-about spots are usually what people are familiar with. We want to look at locations that are popular with locals but do not receive much outside advertising. Although they are not purposely kept a secret, Montrealers frequent these locations for fun. Let me start by telling you that Rue Crescent is a location you should avoid. Although it is a wonderful location, it is also the most crowded with tourists in all of Montreal. You might actually run into someone you know from your home country because it is so touristy. Now, by all means, if that's your thing. But since I pledged to show you all the hot spots frequented by Montrealers, that's what we'll do.

Furco

First up is Furco, which is situated in the heart of the city at 425 Rue Mayor and Rue St. Alexandre. Undoubtedly, your Uber driver is familiar with this location. An older and more professional clientele gradually replaces the younger happy hour patrons in this upmarket wine bar as the evening progresses. With exposed plumbing and bare floorboards, the décor is unusual but elegantly done. You receive a good influx of the office crowd after work because you're in a business area. Come here early in the evening if you want to have a private talk. The sound becomes louder as night falls.

The customers are entertaining, and many of them come to socialize. Summertime is a terrific time to hang out on the terrace, where a DJ plays most nights. The bar offers a wide variety of beverages, and the bartenders are skilled with cocktails. Although they are open from 3 till 5, happy hour doesn't begin until then. At 3 a.m., they close. Cash and credit cards are accepted at Furco, however Apple Pay is not.

Pandore

Another club nearby is Pandore, which is located at 2 Rue Sainte-Catherine E. It's on the fifth story and has views of Montreal's downtown, which is a terrific place to spend an evening in and of itself. The setting is quite posh, and as the last of the dinner guests leave, the partygoers start to mingle. Around 1:00 a.m., when the venue is crowded and busy, it really gets going. Another location where you will have a difficult time finding tourists is this one. Not only is the interior lively, but the terrace and balcony are often packed to the gills, especially on a Friday night. The after-work crowd is present, but the serious partygoers are also present in force.

You may start the night off well by coming here for supper and then getting a head start on the drinks. Don't arrive in a T-shirt because this place is a little dressier. They would let you in, but you would quickly begin to feel uncomfortable. Additionally, you should put on your dancing shoes because this place isn't just noisy for show. There is enough room for everyone on the dance floor, but dancing continues outside on the terrace and in the eating area. Only Thursday, Friday, and Saturday evenings from 4 p.m. to 3 a.m. are this location open.

The latter two are in the heart of the city. The following few are near the Plateau.

Apartment 200

Another favorite hangout among the locals is Apartment 200. The locals recommend it and it's just about having fun and unwinding at the end of a long day, so you won't find it in many tourist publications. On 3643 Boulevard Saint-Laurent, it is just next door to Schwartz's. As a combination of a restaurant and bar, it stands out. The interior is interestingly old, which adds to the atmosphere of the location.

You can actually have a great discussion here while lounging on one of the many couches or playing pool because it's not as noisy as Pandore. It is simultaneously hip and trendy and a lot of fun. The audience fits the atmosphere, and most individuals don't hang out as strangers for very long. It's a fantastic location for networking.

Open daily from 5:00 p.m. to 3:00 a.m. is Apartment 200. Despite having a complete bar, this establishment is not the type where you would want to order elaborate drinks. Shots are fine, as are bottles and drinks on the rocks.

Salon Daomé

On 141 Mont-Royal Avenue E, in Montreal's Le Plateau-Mont-Royal neighborhood, sits Salon Daomé. However, a word of caution: there are no tourists in this area. It's all very Montreal. Everyone may not enjoy the music. To enjoy this location, you must prefer experimental house music. You will be let down if you enter this place with a closed mentality. You will have a lot of fun if you are willing to try new things because the crowd here is, to put it mildly, fascinating. Even though the beverages are inexpensive, if you don't enjoy the style of music, it won't be worth it.

Here, people were free to be themselves and let loose. Dancing is something that will exhaust you if you enjoy it. The DJs here are fairly skilled, and the mirror above the console allows you to observe them spinning. Every night at 10:00, the establishment opens and closes at 3:30. There is a complete bar, but don't anticipate pricey spirits or creative drinks. With the bouncers outside, the pub is quite secure, and you won't see any of the misbehavior that people typically assume takes place. One thing Montrealers are certain of is that this is a town of music. This is evident from the countless music festivals, independent bands, and house music; as a result, it is highly regarded by residents of this magnificent town. Don't be shocked if this ends up being the best experience you've ever had.

Bily Kun

In the Le Plateau-Mont-Royal neighborhood, at 354 Avenue Du Mont-Royal E, is a Czech tavern called Bily Kun. They are available seven days a week from 3 p.m. to 3 a.m. and are rather inexpensive. Drinks are reasonably priced, and the bar is fully stocked with skilled bartenders. They have a wide variety of beer available on tap. Most of the people there are in their twenties and are nice and young. There is plenty of space throughout the week, but on weekends, it becomes packed. So choose between scheduling a busy Thursday visit or a weekend happy hour visit, and then stay. Get a table or stake your claim on a barstool is the key. Although the music is loud, a discussion is not drowned out by it.

Big in Japan

A popular Japanese eatery and bar is located in Japan. On 4175 Boulevard Saint-Laurent, it is situated. Keep it apart from the nearby eatery of the same name. This establishment includes a complete bar with skilled bartenders and an absolutely cozy eating room. They take great satisfaction in having a large assortment of whiskey. As a result, whether you are, or are trying to become, a whiskey expert, this place will suit your needs. Additionally, they serve cocktails that will dazzle you or your date. The meal is unquestionably excellent. Pick up some tuna tataki. You won't regret it, even though it is a little on the pricey side.

Datcha

There is no cover charge before 11:00 p.m., and it is quite well-liked among the residents. Thereafter, it costs roughly $7. There is also no charge for coat check. On Thursday, Friday, Saturday, and Sunday, they open at 10:00 and remain open until three in the morning. They don't operate on other days. With a popular kind of house techno and a solid selection, the music has a young and frantic pace that always keeps the dance floor full. Every now and then, people will bump into each other, and drinks will occasionally spill, which no one seems to mind. It's the cost of having a good time in a busy club.

They are situated at 98 Avenue Laurier O in Plateau Mont Royal. You do not come here to have a conversation. You go there to move about and have fun. There is a full bar, and the drinks are more expensive than average. People are dressed appropriately for the setting here, which implies that nothing is formal but rather that they are stylish and modern and have made an effort to look well. It is not at all carefree. There is a lot of energy, and once you begin going, it would take a zombie to stay still.

Velvet

In this instance, I've saved the finest for last. One of Montreal's top clubs, it is also one of the busiest. Everyone there is between the ages of 21 and 40 and they are all there to party. There is a lot of dancing, drinking, and undoubtedly a lot of hooking up going on. The attendees are experienced partygoers who know how to have a good time. Although some tourists have discovered this place's secret, it is still very much a local hangout. The drinks are good here. Even on a busy night, the bartenders here are quick and serve drinks that are robust.

Location of the club is 426 Rue Saint-Gabriel. They are open from 10:00 p.m. to 2:00 a.m. on Thursday through Saturday. This will cost you a lot of money, so be prepared. This location is by no means affordable. You do, however, get what you pay for. This is not a bar for spectators; here, you enter and engage.

These are the eight clubs in the Montreal area. There are more, but these are the most popular ones because they offer fun activities and aren't overly commercialized. The city of Montreal never sleeps. You can always find something to do till the early hours of the morning.

After a night of dancing and drinking, clubs normally close at around three in the morning, but there is still food available for you to satisfy a stomach that is already empty. The secret ingredient in the entire nightlife scene in Montreal is the caliber of its DJs, along with the enthusiasm of the average Montrealer.

If you intend to party while traveling, arrange your accommodations so that you are close to the action. Your best chance is to stay near the Plateau Mont-Royal or downtown. Although cabs and ridesharing services are readily available at all hours of the night, it is usually preferable to stick close by when you are out partying. Although for the majority of this book it feels like you can just stroll from one end to the other, Montreal is a large metropolis. However, it isn't always the case. To be able to move from one location to the next, you will need to have a mode of transportation planned.

Cultural Festivals

What I refer to as "cultural festivals" is actually a collection of several events that promote Montreal's diverse arts and cultures but don't quite fall into another category. Montreal is teeming with cultural events, from performance art to a festival with a Caribbean theme. From the earliest to the most recent, a few of the more intriguing festivals are as follows:

Wild side Festival

a theatrical festival in which the pieces are chosen from the Fringe Festival winners from the previous year as well as from a number of other foreign and Canadian artists. The plays are performed for the public's delight at the Centaur Theatre and are chosen by a group of professionals. This is a great way to experience Montreal's art scene for individuals who enjoy live theater and performance art.

Biennale de Montréal

For a full month, the Biennale places cutting-edge contemporary art from both the local and global scenes in the center of the urban cultural scene. The relationship between the arts and culture is investigated as society is exposed to initiatives meant to push the envelope. La Biennale is an exhibition of contemporary art that brings together artists from the visual arts, architecture, graphic/object design, music, video, and cinema.

This is a forum for discussion and interaction on many issues affecting the modern art world, and it is also chock full of symposiums and conferences.

Festival TransAmériques (End of May)

The Festival TransAmériques, a gathering together and relatively new event where dance and theatre are at the forefront, encourages open mindedness to the modern arts by drawing attention to interdisciplinary cultural events. This event focuses on exposing the public to creative viewpoints through live exhibitions. The artistic expressions that are produced by directors, choreographers, writers, videographers, and composers are then shown at locations all across the city. The Place-Des-Arts and eleven other locations offer performances. Contact them at (514) 842-0704 or visit their website for the most recent information.

First People's Festival (Mid-June)

This festival, which is held in and around Downtown, offers native-themed arts and crafts, literature, concerts, movies, video, and visual arts. This event is a fantastic method to learn about the Canadian first nations for individuals who are interested in the regional aboriginal culture. Additionally, you can call (514) 572-1799 for more details.

Carifiesta (Early July)

Is it surprising that they established their own festival given the size of the Caribbean community? This celebration, which is centered around a Mardi Gras-style procession and concludes with a spectacle featuring Caribbean music and dancing, is not to be missed. Other festivities are centered on Jean-Drapeau Park, and the free parade is conducted in Downtown Montreal. Call (514) 369-0025, (514) 737-8321, or (514) 334-0270 for more information if you're interested in experiencing Caribbean culture at its finest.

Journées de la culture (End of September)

Throughout the city, Journées de la culture features free events that promote culture. The workshops, visits, and conversations that are part of this festival, which is supported by the government, are all aimed at raising the general public's level of cultural awareness. Buses operated by the STM are available for free public transportation between 9 major stops that are close to more than 140 cultural attractions. This festival is a fun way to spend a few days in September because it's a terrific opportunity to tour the city and be exposed to cultural events.

The Great Pumpkin Ball The Botanical Garden/Jardin Botanique (October)

Every year at the Botanical Garden, a well-known city-sponsored event called The Great Pumpkin Ball is held. The city here organizes a variety of events, including the well-known pumpkin decoration competition. The Ball itself is a display of imaginative pumpkin carvings and decorations made by local artisans rather than a musical dance. Online voting is available for the best carvings. For further information, call (514) 872-1823.

Coup de Coeur Francophone (First Week of November)

French musicians and performers from throughout the world collaborate to spread the French language via music and performances. This festival spans 13 stages with over 90 performances by over 300 performers from near and far. This festival, which focuses on francophone music, is a component of a bigger Canadian occasion. Tickets can be purchased by calling the admission network at (514) 790-1245 for further details. Ticket costs vary depending on the location.

Festival du Monde Arabe de Montréal (FMA) (A Week at the beginning of November)

Even if only for a Week, Arab culture is prominent in Montreal as music, film, dance, and other art forms celebrate its varied manifestations and inspirations. Numerous events are held at more than 12 different locations throughout the city, and given Montreal's abundance of Arab eateries, an entire evening may easily revolve around a particular theme. This event will feature discussions, conferences, movies, calligraphy, flamenco, and Indian-inspired dances. A few performances are free, but others are paid performances in venues like the Medley. Tickets for paid performances can be purchased online at Ticketpro.ca or over the phone at (514) 908-9090.

Salon du Livre (A few days at the end of November)

This event, which is held at Place Bonaventure (800 De La Gauchetière O.; phone: (514) 397-2222), was first held in 1950. Since its start, this event has drawn both children and adults who are fascinated by the world of books of all genres and their publishers. In addition to many scheduled readings, authors will be on hand to sign autographs and sell books. Call (514) 845-2365 for specific information on this festival's admission policies.

Shopping Festivals

Montrealers only have one favorite activity: shopping. There are more shops in the city than I can count, however there are some occasions where you can view the newest trends while occasionally contributing to a good cause. Because of their wide assortment and capacity to provide customers a significant discount compared to what you would pay on a daily basis, the festivals listed below were chosen. Among the more well-known shopping events are:

Salon de L'Amour et de La Séduction (A few days before Valentines Day)

This over-18 shopping festival with a sexual and romantic theme brings together vendors from all over the world at the Olympic

Stadium. Access on a busy Saturday costs around $15, and inside you'll find anything from sexual treats like cakes and chocolates to sex toys and accessories to informational government kiosks on STDs. Additionally, you'll discover retailers of apparel, lingerie, and other sexual accessories. The event is completed with live performances and other activities. You can always phone (450) 928-6969 for further details.

Montréal International Expo Art Festival (A few days at the end of October)

This event, which is held at the Place Bonaventure (800 De La Gauchetière O., (514) 397-2222), offers a venue for contemporary and modern artists to exhibit, exchange, and sell their creations. This event caters to those who enjoy exquisite art and live entertainment. More than 1,000 works of art are on show, created by galleries and artists from throughout the globe. There are works of art for every taste on display in the exhibition area, including photographs, mixed media, ceramics, and sculptures. The price for admittance is $15. You can always call at (514) 907-9321 for further details.

La Braderie de la Mode Québécoise (A few days at the end of October)

This fashion market, which is a well-known Montreal shopping experience, is situated at the Marché Bonsecours in Old Montreal. During the few days that this highly anticipated show is held, designers offer their excess stock and samples, which are mostly geared at women. At this sale, which features over 40 designers, you can receive price reductions ranging from 50% to 80%. You can reach us at (514) 866-2006 for further details. This event, which is a part of Montreal Fashion Week, is most likely the most well-known of the festival's three days of activities.

Au Coeur de la Mode - Farha Foundation (A Sunday in Mid-November)

This charitable event, which is held at the Palais-Des-Congrès, is a fashion show turned retail space. The main focus of this event is fashion for the entire family, and attendees may shop til they drop. The Farha foundation, whose primary goal is to aid in the battle against AIDS, receives 100% of the revenues. At this event, you may get designer clothing and accessories for women, men, and kids at up to 50% off retail prices. A $5 donation is required for entry. Call (514) 270-5010 for further details.

Miscellaneous Festivals

Despite my best efforts to classify every festival in Montreal, certain events just do not fall into any one of the categories I have created. These events comprise:

Grand Ball du Nouvel An

A celebration outside is how some Montrealers prefer to ring in the new year. Forget about the winter and the chilly weather; this festival, which occasionally draws over 40,000 people, is held in the heart of Old Montreal at Place Jacques Cartier. This is a fun, inexpensive way to welcome in the new year and features fireworks, live music, and other events.

Montreal Auto Show (a few days near the end of January)

This annual auto show is a must-see for auto enthusiasts and takes place in the Palais-de-Congress. To showcase upcoming models and industry trends to the public, all the major automakers attend this event. Past and futuristic car concepts are displayed in the exhibits. Themed sections like 7th Heaven (dream automobiles) and the 100% British section are also available. The price of general admission tickets is $15.

Canadian Grand Prix (Mid-June)

The 3-day Formula 1 Grand Prix, which takes place on the Giles Villeneuve racetrack, is typically a bustling event. But at the time this book was being written, the event had just been revived after having been postponed for a year. Although I'm not sure what the new format will be just yet, in the past this event included a race as well as a number of city parties that drew spectators from all around the world. On Crescent, Peel, and St-Laurent streets, various activities are frequently held. These activities include parked F1 racecars, themed games, and free outdoor concerts.

Rogers Cup (End of July, early August, depends on the year)

This tennis competition is held concurrently with the Toronto Tennis competition at the Uniprix Stadium in Parc-Extension, next to Jarry Metro. The finest tennis players in the world compete in both Grand Slam events. Montreal hosts the Men's Tournament one year and the Women's Tournament the following year. In comparison to other tournaments held across the world, tickets are not prohibitively expensive, and you can attempt volunteering to receive a free pass. The finals range in price from $76, to $156 for the 2009 calendar year. Due to the limited seating, exercise caution as they can sell out quickly. You may always reach us at (514) 273-1515, 1-800-678-5440, or 1-800-361-4595 (Canada) (worldwide).

Salon de l'Auto Classique de Montréal (First Weekend of October)

This event is a must-see for any auto enthusiast and is held at the Place Bonaventure (800 De La Gauchetière O., Tel: (514) 397-2222). This one-of-a-kind indoor exhibition showcases a wide range of vehicles, including vintage cars, sports cars, motorcycles, and European models. To take part in the event, custom automobiles and their owners travel as far as New England. Anyone can sign up as an exhibitor if they own a hot rod, muscle car, custom car, restored classic, or foreign sports car. Tickets for the general public are $15 each.

Halloween Frightfest (During the month of October)

The town of La Ronde is overrun by vampires, witches, and other spooky figures for a full month. Children of all ages will enjoy this extra treat to the typical amusement park layout, which is supplemented by live performances by these terrifying animals. Additionally essential is a stop at The Haunted House. The cost of admission is the same as for every other La Ronde visit.

Festival International de Littérature de Montréal (End of September)

Over 2500 writers and artists from Quebec and other countries are featured in this festival, which takes place around the start of the new school year. Even if the Festival is in French, those who enjoy reading should still go. The festival seeks to foster communication between the general population and literature. Live theater, music, cinema, and readings are among the events that take place at locations all across the city. Though certain activities are free to the public, play tickets can cost up to $42. Call (514) 842-2112 for further information if you're interested.

Montreal Fashion Week (For three days in mid-October)

Up-and-coming designers are highlighted during Montreal Fashion Week to the media and industry. The Marché Bonsecours hosts fashion presentations as part of the festival, which is organized as a rival to the Toronto festival of the same name. Additionally, have a look at the Braderie de la Mode Québécoise, which is a fashion-related clearance sale. This fashion experience is open to the public, and tickets may be obtained through the admission network or by phoning (514) 790-1245.

Montreal International ESP Psychic Expo (A Weekend in mid-October)

This weird exhibition/festival, which is held at the Place Bonaventure (800 De La Gauchetière O., (514) 397-2222), brings together psychics, astrologers, clairvoyants, and other "professionals" of the occult and new age genre. All of these experts get together at the Place Bonaventure to provide you with one-of-a-kind experiences and activities including free talks and demonstrations where you may discover a little more about yourself and the paranormal. You can always phone (514) 341-6290 for further details. General entry is $10.

Chapter 9: Souvenirs And Shopping in Montreal

It makes sense to wish to preserve a memory of your vacation to Montreal, a city renowned for its vivacious history, distinctive charm, and rich culture. This essay will examine 15 outstanding Montreal souvenirs that perfectly capture the spirit of this alluring city. You'll find a wide variety of souvenirs that will serve as an enduring remember of your time in Montreal, from handcrafted jewelry to classic Canadian foods.

Artisan Jewelry

A thriving group of talented artists that produce magnificent jewelry with painstaking craftsmanship may be found in Montreal. These artisans create hand-made, one-of-a-kind items that perfectly capture Montreal's artistic character, drawing inspiration from the city's rich tradition and the appeal of certified Canadian diamonds. Artisan jewelry from Montreal offers for a genuinely unique keepsake, whether it's a dazzling ring, delicate earrings, a chic bracelet, or a classic necklace. The renowned Bonsecours Market in Old Montreal, a haven for regional craftspeople and a must-visit location for anyone looking for distinctive and heartfelt mementos, is where you may find these gems.

Quebec Cheeses

Montreal, which has a strong French past and a passion for food, is a cheese lover's dream come true. Quebec is known for producing outstanding cheese that comes in a wide variety of flavors and textures. Quebec cheeses may enhance any dining experience, whether it is robust and sour or smooth and creamy. Several well-known regional brands include Trois-Pistoles, Saint-Benoît, Saint-Paulin, and Oka. Visit Fromagerie Hamel at the Jean-Talon Market if you want to become fully immersed in the world of Quebec cheeses. Your server's expert advice can help you choose the perfect wine or beer pairings from all the tempting options.

Maple Products

A trip to Canada wouldn't be complete without indulging in some of its famous maple-based treats. A variety of delicious sweets produced with maple syrup are available in Quebec, which is Canada's top producer of the sweetener. You'll find a great choice of options to sate your sweet craving, including maple-infused beverages as well as maple-infused candies, cookies, and syrup itself. As a tasty memento of your time in Montreal, bring a bottle of genuine Quebec maple syrup or a box of chocolates fashioned like maple leaves home.

Winter Accessories

The frigid winters in Montreal necessitate attractive yet useful winter gear. Find warm and fashionable hats, scarves, and gloves made of premium materials like wool and cashmere by browsing the city's shops and markets. These accessories not only keep you warm but also infuse your clothing with a little of Montreal's distinct sense of style.

Bagels

The famed and well-known Montreal bagels are known for their peculiar chewy texture and sweet, somewhat smokey flavor. The practice of baking these hand-rolled treats in wood-fired ovens extends back to the city's early immigrant families. Take a bag of Montreal bagels home with you from famous shops like

Fairmount Bagel or St-Viateur Bagel, and you may continue to enjoy their distinctive flavor long after your trip.

Canadian Coins

Montreal presents a great opportunity to add some Canadian money to your collection if you enjoy collecting coins from various nations. Obtain a selection of Canadian coins, including special editions that celebrate important moments in Canadian history and have distinctive designs. These coins offer interesting conversation starters and act as a tangible memento of your experience in Canada.

The Bay Point Blanket

An iconic representation of Canadian heritage and craftsmanship is the Hudson's Bay Point Blanket. This blanket, which is made entirely of wool, has characteristic multistripes in vivid hues that evoke the old trading blankets once used by fur traders. The Bay Point Blanket is a treasured heritage that captures the essence of Canada in addition to being a cozy and useful item. To relive your experience in Montreal, wrap yourself with this iconic blanket or use it as decor in your house.

Ice Wine and Cider

The climate in Quebec is perfect for making superb ice wines and ciders. Grapes that have been naturally frozen on the vine are used to make ice wine, which has a lusciously sweet and powerful flavor. Another well-liked local delicacy is cider, which shows the apple orchards in the area and comes in a variety of flavors and styles. Take a sip of Quebec's abundant fruit by purchasing a bottle of ice wine or cider from one of Montreal's specialized shops.

Roots Canada Clothing

Famously producing fashionable and high-quality apparel, Roots Canada is a Canadian company. Roots offers a variety of clothing that perfectly encapsulates Canadian style, from warm sweaters and jackets to soft loungewear. Visit one of their shops in Montreal and take home a garment that blends style, coziness, and a hint of Canadian heritage.

Local Beers

Locally brewed beers are a terrific memento for beer fans because to Montreal's thriving craft beer culture, which has attracted attention on a global scale. Explore breweries and brewpubs all across the city to sample a wide variety of flavors, styles, and innovative brewing methods. Craft beers from Montreal offer a glimpse of the artistic essence of the city, ranging from hop-forward IPAs to rich stouts and crisp ales.

Canned Foods

Although canned foods might not be the first thing that springs to mind when considering souvenirs, Montreal has a variety of mouthwatering canned treats that are ideal for taking home. Find unusual sauces, smoked salmon, pickled veggies, and other canned items that reflect the city's culinary diversity by perusing neighborhood markets and specialized food shops. Long after your trip is over, you can still enjoy these canned goods because they give you a taste of Montreal's flavors.

Aboriginal Handicraft

Numerous forms of art and handicrafts honor Canada's rich Indigenous heritage. Beautifully created Aboriginal objects, such as traditional sculptures, jewelry, dream catchers, and pottery, are available in Montreal. These one-of-a-kind works of art have deep cultural meaning and provide a window into Canada's many Indigenous traditions.

Tim Hortons Coffee

Popular Canadian coffee shop chain Tim Hortons has ingrained itself in Canadian culture. You may enjoy the taste of Canada's most well-liked coffee in the comfort of your own home by bringing a bag of Tim Hortons coffee beans home. Tim Hortons coffee will take you back to the warm and welcome ambiance of a Tim Hortons cafe with its smooth and rich flavor.

Hockey Memorabilia

The historic Montreal Canadiens, one of the most prosperous and recognizable clubs in the National Hockey League, are based in

Montreal and have a special position in Canadian culture as a result. Find hockey memorabilia, such as jerseys, pucks, or autographed photos, in souvenir shops and sports shops to take a piece of Montreal's hockey history with you.

Other Interesting Souvenirs from Canada:

1. **Inukshuk:** Traditionally constructed by the Inuit people, an inukshuk is a stone building that depicts a human form. It stands for advice, companionship, and hope. Consider bringing home a miniature Inukshuk replica as a sentimental and noteworthy gift.

2. **Smoked British Columbia Salmon:** Salmon from British Columbia is renowned for being of the highest quality, and smoked salmon is a specialty that highlights the area's culinary prowess. To appreciate the smoked salmon's complex flavor and send a piece of the West Coast back home, buy vacuum-sealed packs.

3. **Dream Catchers:** Native American dream catchers are intricately crafted objects that are said to screen out negative dreams while letting only happy dreams in. These exquisite and profound works of art make for compelling keepsakes that lend a sense of spirituality to any setting.

You can preserve the priceless memories and adventures of your journey by bringing a souvenir from Montreal home. The wide range of mementos embodies the spirit of Montreal's culture, history, and gastronomic delights, from artisan jewelry and Quebec cheeses to maple products and one-of-a-kind handicrafts. Each item, whether it be a physical remembrance or a delicious treat, serves as a reminder of the exciting and alluring city of Montreal. In order to take a piece of Montreal home with you when you plan your next trip, keep in mind to look through these extraordinary keepsakes and select the ones that speak to you.

Chapter 10:
Tips For Traveling in Montreal

Is Montréal worth visiting?

In a nutshell, the answer to this question is without a doubt, yes! Heart of Canada's shining gem is Montréal. This city frequently has the reputation of being Canada's cool kid, which attracts tourists in a distinctive way1. The city is a fusion of genuine European elegance, vibrant culture, amiable locals, and a rainbow of artistic talent and scenic beauty.

Montréal is popular for its cafe scene, picnics in the park way of life, and magnificent architecture, all of which add to its allure. Montréal is more than just a city; it is a miniature world of people, color, and charisma.

Things to know before going to Montréal, Canada

The trip experience can be improved by familiarizing oneself with local traditions and laws before traveling there. In the multilingual city of Montréal, French and English are the two main spoken languages. Visitors may get by with just English despite having one of the greatest French-speaking populations in the world.

The city has a bustling food scene, plenty of greenery, distinctive architecture, and a rich cultural past. Visitors to Montréal can more easily navigate the city thanks to the effective metro system that links the downtown to the main tourist attractions.

Tips for Your First Trip to Montreal

Use transit to get around and save money

With a network of bus and metro lines spanning the size of the city, Montréal is home to an amazing public transportation system. These solutions offer city exploration that is both affordable and effective. Tourists can take as many rides as they want within a set time window thanks to the integrated fare system.

You can't turn right on a red light

The inability to turn right on a red signal in Montréal is an odd but important traffic law. To avoid any unwarranted fines, keep in mind this advice.

The city is bilingual

The city of Montréal takes pride in its bilingualism. Despite English being the most common language, French is the most widely spoken. However, it wouldn't hurt to know a few French proverbs.

5-à-7 means happy hour

In Montréal, happy hour is known as "5-à-7." Typically from 5 to 7 pm, most bars and restaurants offer drink specials at this time.

The legal drinking age is 18

In Montréal, the drinking age is 18, as opposed to many other places. This aspect makes it possible for younger visitors to enjoy the city's exciting nightlife.

North isn't really north

For newcomers, the city's distinctive orientation can be a little perplexing. What is typically referred to as "north" in Montréal is actually "north-east." When navigating across the city, keep this advice in mind.

A "dep" is a convenience store

The word "depanneur," which means a convenience store in English, is short for "dépanneur" in French. These shops are commonplace in Montréal and are trusted sources for requirements.

Save money with a Museums Card

There are many museums in Montréal, each of which provides a distinctive perspective on a range of subjects. Consider getting a Museums Card to avoid paying admission costs. This card offers discounted entrance to a number of sites.

Take a free walking tour

Join a free walking tour to learn more about the city's fascinating history and culture. Major locations are frequently covered on these trips, which also offer fascinating historical accounts of Montréal.

BYOW restaurants

One of the few cities with a BYOW (Bring Your Own Wine) option is Montréal. Many restaurants let patrons bring their own wine, making for a distinctive dining experience.

Montréal is more than just a place to visit; it is an encounter that stays in the hearts of travelers. Utilizing the aforementioned advice will make traveling this attractive city a snap.

Conclusion

Let's pause to take in the diverse and lively landscape that is the center of French-speaking Canada as we draw the curtain on this educational tour of Montreal and Quebec. We set out on this voyage to solve the puzzles, delve into the past, and discover the rich culture that these places have.

We explored the multicultural side of Montreal, the second-largest French-speaking metropolis in the world after Paris, as part of the "Montreal and Quebec Travel Guide." We investigated Montreal's French accent, which harmoniously mingled with the tongues of 80 other ethnic populations to produce a medley of languages and cultures that gave the city its special appeal. A city brimming with life, history, and culture is encapsulated by its combination of Old-World elegance and North American vigor.

We made our way through Old Montreal's bustling streets, which are located in the city's oldest district and feature cobblestone lanes, old buildings, public squares, and monuments. Our journey took on a more spiritual quality thanks to the aura of the Notre-Dame Basilica, a neo-gothic masterpiece and the gem in the crown of Quebec's extensive religious legacy. We also went on a tour of the historic Old Port, a bustling neighborhood with a wide range of attractions, shops, art galleries, cafes, restaurants, and museums.

Inviting us to cruise the promenade in front of the Chateau Frontenac and visit La Citadelle, Quebec City, a UNESCO World Heritage Site, welcomed us with open arms. Our investigation was aided by knowledgeable tips and suggestions, expertly selected maps, and practical terms and phrases in Quebecois that enabled us to go deeply into the city's core.

As we looked back on our tour, we confidently fulfilled our commitment to provide an authentic guide that presents the spirit of Montreal and Quebec. The guide has been carefully chosen to enhance your travel experience, make trip planning easier, and help you get the most out of your time. The top attractions, eateries, lodgings, nightlife, shopping, performing arts, activities, and side trips are all expertly woven into this intricate tapestry of historical and cultural insights, practical advice that can't be overstated, and honest recommendations.

Last but not least, if there is one thing we want you to remember from this guide, it is that Montreal and Quebec are at their best when they combine their ancient elegance with contemporary vitality. It is a symbol of unity in diversity, the peaceful cohabitation of various cultures, and the vivacious spirit that permeates its streets, cafes, restaurants, and residents. And the distinct language and culture of Quebecois are how Canada's spirit is conveyed.

We think this guide has accomplished its goal of igniting your wanderlust, whether you're a history buff, a culture vulture, a foodie, or just an avid traveler. So be sure to include this information along with your belongings when you pack for Montreal and Quebec. It will serve as your guide, vocabulary, navigator, and window into the heart of French-speaking Canada.

Au revoir and happy travels!

Made in the USA
Middletown, DE
11 July 2023

34878759R00060